LOVE
LINES
MARK
ANTHONY

A good heart deserves a good home.

Mark Anthony

You
deserve
a
love
for
all
times,
especially
hard
times.

Mark Anthony

3

You
make
my
day
just
by
being
you.

Mark Anthony

Most
happy
endings
begin
after
a
terrible
goodbye.

Mark Anthony

She
isn't
lonely
she
is
just
waiting
for
the right one
to
come
along.

I
wasn't
interested
in
her
temporary
only
her
forever.

Mark Anthony

Listen
to
her.
Feed
her.
Kiss
her.
Love
her.
Never
leave
her.

Mark Anthony

Broken
hearted
girls
become
women
warriors
who
can
change
the
world.

Don't
lose
sleep
over
somebody
who
doesn't
dream
of
you.

If
he's
not
making
the
effort
he's
not
worth
your
time.

Mark Anthony

Find somebody who shares your definition of love.

Mark Anthony

I
will
never
stop
being
the one
who
always
wants
more
of
you.

She's
easy
to
love
because
she's
the
one.

Mark Anthony

All
I need
is a
little
bit
of you
in my
day
to
make
me
smile.

Mark Anthony

She
is
rare
because
she
is
real.

Mark Anthony

Just
when
I
thought
love
wasn't
for
me,
then
along
came
you.

She will listen to your words, but your actions will say more.

She
finally
fell
in
love
with
someone
who
can
handle
her
fire.

She
wants
a
love
that's
wild
and
a
heart
that's
true.

Mark Anthony

I've
fallen
in
love
a
few
times
but
only
stayed
in love
with you.

In
you,
I
find
the
best
part
of
myself.

You
deserve
all
the
dreams
you
keep
hidden
in
your
heart.

Mark Anthony

Love
her
and
let
her
bloom.

Mark Anthony

The answer is still love.

Mark Anthony

One
day
you'll
be with
the one
you're
meant
to be with,
and
the rest
will be
history.

Love
with
her
is
always
easy,
even
when
it's
hard.

Mark Anthony

Actions speak louder than words, so kiss her like you mean it.

Mark Anthony

It
doesn't
matter
where
I am,
my dear,
if you're
with me,
it's
a
beautiful
place.

Mark Anthony

I
found
you
without
looking
and
love
you
without
trying.

Mark Anthony

Patience
my
dear,
in
all
things,
but
especially
in
love.

All
she
wanted
was
a
love
that
brought
out
the
best
in her.

Mark Anthony

First,
understand
your
worth.
Second
don't
settle
for
less.

Beauty
comes
in
many
forms,
but
you
are
my
favorite.

Mark Anthony

So
many
people
in
this
world,
yet
I'm
madly
in love
with
you.

She
survived
the
worst
in
order
to
become
her
best.

Some relationships teach us what we don't want, some teach us we can have it all.

Mark Anthony

She's worth whatever chaos she brings to the table and you know it.

Mark Anthony

38

Promise me, you'll never stop dreaming of us.

Mark Anthony

The
right
one
will
never
feel
wrong.

Mark Anthony

Find someone who shares your definition of love.

Mark Anthony

Her
smile
reminded
me
of
what
happiness
looks
like.

Mark Anthony

One
day
someone
will
light
a match
inside
of you
that
will
burn
forever.

Real
love
stays
because
there
is
no
place
else
it
wants
to be.

You
deserve
somebody
who
knows
your
soul
and
protects
your
heart.

Choose
the one
who
chooses
you
above
all
others
and
knows
exactly
why.

Everything
happens
for
a
reason,
including
us.

Mark Anthony

I
always
hoped
I'd
end
up
with
someone
exactly
like
you.

My favorite humans are the ones who let me be as crazy as I am.

Mark Anthony

I
believe
you
will
always
find
a
way
to
love.

Mark Anthony

She
found
the
courage
to
move
on,
and
a heart
ready
for
real love.

Mark Anthony

You
deserve
to
feel
loved
and
appreciated
for
who
you
are.

She
is the
kind of
woman
you
read
about
in poems,
yet she is
as real
as real
can be.

You're
the
one
I
waited
for,
the
one
I
can't
deny.

Mark Anthony

Find the one that wants to show you off.

There comes a time, when only a soulmate will do.

Mark Anthony

The
right
one
is
you.

Mark Anthony

Believe in her until she remembers to believe in herself.

Mark Anthony

Missing
each
other
is
all
part
of
the
magic.

Mark Anthony

Thank
you
for
being
you
in
a
world
full
of
somebody
else's.

Mark Anthony

Everybody
said
we
were
lost
but
somehow
our
love
found
a
way.

Mark Anthony

You
won't
meet
your
soulmate
until
you're
both
ready
to say
hello
forever.

Mark Anthony

He
was
part
of
your
story
but
not
your
happily
ever
after.

Heartbreak teaches us to take care of fragile things.

She is
worth
the
wait.
She is
worth
the
time.
She is
the
reason
why.

Mark Anthony

She
was
her
own
muse.

Mark Anthony

You
are
the fire
in my
veins,
the wild
in my
heart,
the
sunset
in my
soul.

Mark Anthony

She
was
her
own
muse.

Mark Anthony

I
loved
her
from
the
moment
I
heard
my
first
love
story.

Mark Anthony

Souls
like
ours
travel
lifetimes
just
to
see
each
other
again.

Mark Anthony

I
waited
my
entire
life
and
you
were
worth
every
minute.

Mark Anthony

All
I
need—
the stars,
the moon,
the sea
and
your
hand
in
mine.

Mark Anthony

Her
scars
are a
beautiful
map
of
her
past
that
led
her
to me.

Mark Anthony

Nothing
brings
me
to
life
faster
than
you.

Mark Anthony

Her
scars
are a
beautiful
map
of
her
past
that
led
her
to me.

Mark Anthony

Nothing brings me to life faster than you.

You
are
not
your
anxiety
or
fear.
You are
the one
who
rises
above.

You
will
always
be
the
light
that
shows
me
the
way
home.

Mark Anthony

B7

CPSIA information can be obtained
at www.ICGtesting.com
Printed in the USA
BVHW030138021020
590086BV00004B/156